MASTER
YOUR FEARS

Cover design by: Ebbony E. Doty
Cover photo by: Danny Kang Austin

ISBN: 978-1-959095-29-3   2 3 4 5 6 7 8 9 10

Printed in the United States of America

Kings Take
Serpents
by the Tail

MASTER
YOUR FEARS

Stephen A. Davis

K

KUDU

DEDICATION

To God: The source of my wisdom, strength, and

passion to be able to lead such great people.

To my wife, Michelle Darlene Davis: You are my

greatest and most loving cheerleader in life, and I thank

you for always encouraging and praying for me.

There is so much more – watch this. I love you!

To my children: Sasha, Amber, and April, you

are my absolute joy whom I love dearly.

Thank you for your love and support

in continuing this legacy.

CONTENTS

Foreword ix

Introduction xiii

CHAPTER 1: **Fear Can Become A Tool** 17

CHAPTER 2: **I'm Done Fleeing!** 27

CHAPTER 3: **Don't Leave Your Rod** 35

CHAPTER 4: **Power From Within** 45

CHAPTER 5: **Arise, Jump, and Dismantle!** 55

CHAPTER 6: **Expect Great Results** 63

FOREWORD

I n a world frozen by fear, this book equips us to rise above it. We know some of our fears, and we see them used against us by the powers in this fallen world as venom in the fangs of a deadly serpent, killing our effectiveness for the kingdom of God. Other fears hide deep within ourselves—within our past or our outlooks; it requires a brave heart to pull back the layers of our lives and examine them fully. Bishop Stephen Davis helps us do just this. He knows we can live bigger than our fear, and live with greater significance.

For many years, in leadership meetings around the nation, I have taught, "When you become a leader, you lose the right to think about yourself." It's a phrase I have used over and over to try to communicate the true heart of leadership. A selfish leader will find themselves leading no one. To be an effective leader, you must stop any form of selfishness and do what is best for others. This kind of effective leadership requires a servant's heart. Deepening the meaning of this thought, Bishop Davis teaches us in this book that thinking selflessly as a leader requires us to face our fears—even the deeply rooted ones. By facing our fears on behalf of others, we will find our leadership skills increasing, our dependence on the Heavenly Father increasing, and our effectiveness and significance as leaders flourishing.

Bishop Davis has lived his life exhibiting this type of selfless leadership. He is always willing to do the difficult work required to lead effectively. He is an example we all can follow and learn from, and the wisdom he shares in this book will be a gift to all who read it.

Bishop Davis digs far into Scripture, weaving together truth after truth, explaining how the Bible's greatest leaders faced their fears and found victory. He focuses on Moses and his approach to fear, and we learn how deep fear can go—even for those of us with years of experience. Far more than being informed, we are equipped to fight the fears we find hiding in our lives with practical truths.

A fearful leader is not an effective leader, and we must do what we have to do to take hold of any fear strongholds in our lives and eradicate them, leaning on the Father to help us do so. When we do, we will see how powerful a God we serve: He can take the very things we are afraid of and use them for His glory. As you read the pages ahead, do so with an open heart and a selfless mindset. Facing your fear isn't easy, and neither is effective leadership... but both are critical in a world gripped by fear.

Dr. Gerald Brooks

Pastor of Grace Outreach Center in Plano, Texas

INTRODUCTION

What is fear?

Fear is defined by the Merriam-Webster Dictionary as "an unpleasant often strong emotion caused by anticipation or awareness of danger."[1] In this definition, there are keywords that we can look at to address the root of fear. 1) Emotion, 2) Anticipation, 3) Awareness, and 4) Danger. There may have been situations you faced that were unpleasant which left a mark in your mind, thoughts, and emotions. The next time something occurs that resembles that unpleasant situation, you then perceive it as a threat.

---

1 Merriam-Webster.com Dictionary, s.v. "fear," accessed December 12, 2022, https://www.merriam-webster.com/dictionary/fear.

We hear about it and have even experienced it, but what is it, really? Always understand that fear is a challenge in every person's life and not an isolated occurrence. Psychologically, it is difficult to believe that what you may have once feared can be used as a tool of advantage against your opposition. In other words, fear can be a weapon used against you or for your advancement.

Dr. Caroline Leaf in her book, "Who Switched Off My Brain", shared that every time a memory is built there is also a corresponding emotion.[2] Memory and emotions are like body and mind – inseparable. So, if a situation is perceived as a threat, whether real or imagined, it triggers a response which often is to flee. The universal trigger for fear is the threat of harm. This threat, however, can be to our physical, emotional, or psychological well-being.

Maybe it's time to take another look at the situation you perceived as a threat that caused you to flee in the other

---

2 Leaf, Caroline. *Who Switched off My Brain?: Controlling Toxic Thoughts and Emotions.* Southlake, TX: Inprov, Ltd., 2009.

direction and see if that is your calling even if you are afraid of it.

This book will teach you how to take control of what you fear and channel it for the advancement of those around you. My passion is to help you realize that you have purpose and a God-given potential. You will learn how to awaken your potential and stand firm in the face of adversity, even fear.

You will learn that Kings take serpents by the tail - master your fears!

CHAPTER 1

FEAR CAN BECOME A TOOL

God created us like no other creatures on earth. To understand the significance of our existence is to begin a life that dominates our current fears. We have grown up with certain views of our surroundings—views that paralyze us from seizing opportunities and being solutions to major problems in society. Many of our fears point to the fact that we are each an answer to the question of how a specific group of people can overcome.

Your willingness to overcome your fears will lead to the most rewarding achievement in your existence. Always understand that fear is a challenge in every person's life—not an isolated occurrence. Those who are accomplishing great things in life have chosen to take hold of their fears and use them as weapons to transform the world in which they live. I can personally say that the things I feared became tools to advance me—and thousands who choose to yield to my teaching and instructions. Over the years, I haven't done what I felt most comfortable doing; instead, I've done things I never saw as my "strengths." Maybe it's time to take another look at what caused you to flee in the other direction. Maybe it's time to evaluate if the thing you fled from is truly your calling—yes, even if you are afraid of it.

> *Then Moses answered and said, "But suppose they will not believe me or listen to my voice; suppose they say, 'The Lord has not appeared to you.'"*
>
> *So the Lord said to him, "What is that in your hand?"*
>
> *He said, "A rod."*
>
> *And He said, "Cast it on the ground."*

So he cast it on the ground, and it became a serpent;

and Moses fled from it.

Then the LORD said to Moses, "Reach out your hand

and take it by the tail" (and he reached out his hand

and caught it, and it became a rod in his hand),

"that they may believe that the LORD God of their

fathers, the God of Abraham, the God of Isaac, and

the God of Jacob, has appeared to you."

—*Exodus 4:1-5 (NKJV)*

Many times, we don't seize upon a thought or idea because of fear. This can be the case whether the thought or idea is from God or an image from a person's imagination. Moses is a great example of someone who is given an opportunity but is arrested by fear. Like Moses, we have to be shown that there is nothing to fear when the thing near to you changes its form.

YOUR WILLINGNESS TO OVERCOME YOUR FEARS WILL LEAD TO THE MOST REWARDING ACHIEVEMENT IN YOUR EXISTENCE.

Any apparent problem has the potential to become an answer, even if it is a serpent. It is difficult to believe that what you once may have feared can be used as a tool of advantage against your opposition. As we look into this scripture, we find that something amazing lies just beyond our fears. Moses's courage to take the serpent by the tail would impact three-and-a-half million people. The moment Moses confronted his fears was the moment a series of victories began—and the moment the freedom of God's people became inevitable. The thing you are afraid of has meaning when it relates to the forces that are restraining society from moving forward.

Let's take a closer look at the symbolism of the serpent and the rod—what they represented in that day. Numbers 21:8-9 (NKJV) gives us a broader view into the use of the serpent:

> Then the LORD said to Moses, "Make a fiery serpent, and set it on a pole; and it shall be that everyone who is bitten, when he looks at it, shall live." So Moses made a bronze serpent, and put it on a pole; and so it was, if a serpent had bitten anyone, when he looked at the bronze serpent, he lived.

The Israelite people knew the serpent as a symbol of divination or fortune-telling while they were enslaved by the Egyptians. It was also an emblem worn by Pharaoh on his headwear. In these two instances, the serpent was displayed as a source of power. Never allow images or things that resemble the past to create moments of fear that prevent you from advancing forward. I have come to realize that for every evil power there is a greater power that exists for the good of our society.

The rod, which had the ability to transform in the hands of Moses, was a source of miraculous power and healing. Through Moses's conquest, the rod was used numerous times to demonstrate the power of God that rested upon it. The rod also served as a scepter of rule and authority. A scepter is a representation of royal power and authority or sovereignty. Moses used the rod to bring water out of a rock, to open up the Red Sea and to gain victory over the Amalekites. Now, we can see the importance of Moses overcoming his fear of the rod: it carried so much significance for the journey before him and his people.

Let's look at some items that carry great importance when it comes to the journey before us:

Don't let fear stop you from taking the serpent by the tail. By now, you may know what your serpent is—the thing you fear that needs to be taken by the tail. Something in life has challenged each of us, bringing us discomfort or fear. Fleeing is not the answer to every frightening thing we encounter in life; instead, we must stand, knowing there is some good in most bad things.

1. *God is going to use what you were afraid of as proof of your encounter with Him.* For many years, God has used our weaknesses and fears to reveal to us a power that is also close to us.

2. *When you take the serpent by the tail, it seals your victory.* It takes many of us time to overcome the things we fear. However, once we choose to confront the fear, a world of victories is released into our lives. Fear is usually consuming one area of our lives that impacts multiple other areas at any given time. So once we have achieved one victory, many other victories become part of our day-to-day experience.

3. *Take every harmful force by the tail.* There is an inner liberation that takes place once a person finds the

courage to stare at an obstacle that for many years has blocked them in life. Those who dare to come face-to-face with what seems like a harmful experience—and arise in victory—will soon take on a fearless posture in all encounters.

4. *Healing is in what you were bitten by.* From the venom of everything which bites a person to harm them, a serum of healing can be created.

NOTES

CHAPTER 2

I'M DONE FLEEING!

Moses fled for his life from Pharaoh. Exodus 2:15 (NKJV) says, "When Pharaoh heard of this matter, he sought to kill Moses. But Moses fled from the face of Pharaoh and dwelt in the land of Midian; and he sat down by a well."

Fleeing is often the first response of those who have been called to a great work that will change the lives of many people. Moses was not the first to flee, and he was not the last, either. Some of us, like Moses, have created a pattern of fleeing. It is a common reaction when you are afraid or don't completely understand something.

In the same manner as Moses had fled from the serpent, he fled from Pharaoh. Very early in life, we begin to establish healthy—or destructive—patterns. These patterns can be so destructive, in fact, that they cause us to miss our destiny. Groups of people can perish as a result of this. I believe God wants to correct this fleeing issue in us today just as he did with Moses. Let's look a little closer at the situation.

Exodus 4:3 (NKJV) says, "And He said, 'Cast it on the ground.' So he cast it on the ground, and it became a serpent; and Moses fled from it." Everything God gives us has the ability to change its form. When Moses cast the rod to the ground, its form changed from a rod into a serpent, which demonstrates the ability that lies within an object given by God. Moses was not aware of the potential in the rod he was carrying, so he was afraid. God created everything with the inner ability to increase or change in form. We have not fully investigated the things that have been placed within our reach, and therefore we have a tendency to fear what we have not explored. Fear is a normal reaction to what we do not quite understand. But what Moses was afraid of actually became his weapon—the thing that brought him a great victory. It is possible to be afraid of the very power for which you have been searching.

Moses was trying to flee from his calling. Exodus 3:11 (NKJV) reads, "But Moses said to God, "Who am I that I should go to Pharaoh, and that I should bring the children of Israel out of Egypt?" Much like Moses, many of us who carry special talents and abilities tend to flee from the assignment placed on our lives. It is never easy to say yes to a purpose larger than you; but fleeing is not the answer. Many lives are always at stake when purpose comes to confront us. You are not the first one that desired to flee, and you will not be the last. We all can make a choice to be an example to many, just as Moses is to us. Overcoming your fear will minimize your fleeing and secure your purpose for existence.

There is no record of Moses fleeing again after taking hold of the serpent that became a rod in his hand. As we see through his example, once you take hold of what you fear by the tail, a great level of confidence will invade your life, resulting in a daily decline of the temptation to flee. Now that we have a better knowledge of what causes flight, we can address the fear that has been designed to cancel our purpose. Untold opportunities are before you, so fleeing is no longer an option.

GOD DOESN'T HAVE A PROBLEM WITH YOU BEING AFRAID, BUT HE DOES HAVE A PROBLEM WITH YOU QUITTING.

Once you take hold of what hurt you or made you afraid, you will face every challenge head-on. You have the ability to take control of what you fear and channel it for the advancement of those around you. Many others have experienced hurt, and they struggle daily with fear; but the victory you achieve will be the living example for them. The more people can clearly see leadership overcoming fear, the more they will stimulate their desires for higher levels of living. Moses's example was a lesson: you can pick up what scared you, because you will need it for where you are going. There is a miracle in what you pick up, and the things you have to pick up are the things you left alone because of fear.

Just like Moses couldn't lead people out of captivity until he picked up the serpent, you can't lead people to the other side of their captivity if you never pick up your serpent. It will be clear when you have picked something up—you'll display the backbone to stand firm in the midst of adversities and trials. God doesn't have a problem with you being afraid, but He does have a problem with you quitting.

Everything you have been afraid of has prepared you for right now. What you have gone through was a necessary tool to remove fear from your path. When God tells you to do something you do not want to do, know that He has a training method in mind that will benefit you. All the things that made you afraid were good for you. Psalm 119:71 (NKJV) says, "It is good for me that I have been afflicted, that I may learn Your statutes."

Every time you flee, you have to start over. *I'm done fleeing*! You can be scared, afraid, or hurt—just don't run. When you come to the point at which you're no longer afraid, you will actually begin to torment your opposition. You have to make up your mind that you're finished fleeing. God knew you were going to have to pick up things that you previously feared—that's why He placed greatness in you. There will be times and seasons in which you are without understanding, but *do not flee*. One of my famous quotes is "Your understanding can wait, but your obedience cannot."

NOTES

CHAPTER 3

DON'T LEAVE YOUR ROD

Then the LORD spoke to Moses and Aaron, saying, "When

Pharaoh speaks to you, saying, 'Show a miracle for

yourselves,' then you shall say to Aaron, 'Take your rod

and cast it before Pharaoh, and let it become a serpent.'"

Exodus 7:8-9 (NKJV)

The authority and power of the rod were important demonstrations of God's power to Pharaoh. Moses and Aaron entered an environment of soothsayers who were working magic on behalf of Pharaoh. The supernatural was being demonstrated through the darkness of Pharaoh's magicians. Therefore, there needed to be a supernatural power that accompanied those sent by God.

Magic is a manipulation of the mind, but the supernatural power wielded by Moses was a revelation of God's power. With this power, Moses revealed the strength of God in the midst of the children of Israel. They were more in number than the Egyptians but lacked the ability to believe for freedom from Pharaoh's bondage. They were a greater army than the Egyptians, but Pharaoh had confined them mentally, not physically. The magicians used magic to enslave the people. God's miracles were used by Moses to free the people.

The only way people can be free, get their attention back on God and see miracles is through the leadership of those who believe in God's supernatural power. The rod represented miracles, which are wrought through the supernatural. Take hold of what you are running from and lead with miracles that bring forth freedom. Physically, you may never see the rod, but all who look to you will feel and see its impact. Symbolically, you're grabbing hold of a rod which stimulates your faith that you will bring deliverance to an oppressed people. It's important to understand that magic is of darkness and manipulation. Miracles are of God and represent the light.

The rod was a sign that God would do miracles to save his people. Take a look at what Jesus says in Mark 16:17-18 (NKJV):

"And these signs will follow those who believe: in My name they will cast out demons; they will speak with new tongues;

they will take up serpents; and if they drink anything deadly, it will by no means hurt them; they will lay hands on the sick, and they will recover."

We still have the potential to take up what could hurt us and, through our faith in God, see the serpent become a rod each time. The rod is always be a sign of your authority and position, so never do anything without it.

Moses's rod was for leading God's people out of Egypt—it wasn't to save Egypt. Take a look at Exodus 4:19-21 (NKJV):

"Now the Lord said to Moses in Midian, 'Go, return to Egypt; for all the men who sought your life are dead.' Then Moses took his wife and his sons and set them on a donkey, and he returned to the land of Egypt. And Moses took the rod of God in his hand.

And the LORD said to Moses, 'When you go back to Egypt, see that you do all those wonders before Pharaoh which I have put in your hand. But I will harden his heart, so that he will not let the people go.'"

God wants to remove us from some systems of this world because He has no plans to fix them. God was not interested in fixing Egypt; His focus was bringing His people out of the land. The thing you are trying to fix just may be something God doesn't want fixed. So listen very

closely to His voice—He may just be calling you out of it.
Don't spend all your time working on something God has
no intention on fixing. It may not be working because God
is trying to get you out of it!

WHENEVER YOU HAVE PURPOSE WITHOUT TRAINING, IT CREATES ROOM FOR FAILURE. KNOW THE DIFFERENCE BETWEEN YOUR STRENGTH AND GOD'S.

Have you ever thought about the fact that you may be
trying to stay and fix a place that God is ultimately plan-
ning to destroy? God sent Moses back to Egypt once the
influence of the previous ruling Pharaoh was gone. God
is going to send you back on a rescue mission to deliver
those oppressed by the same thing from which you have

been delivered. Whenever the enemy seems persistent, God is facilitating His plan to overthrow that enemy. Don't give up when things aren't moving the way you want them to move. Anything that is fighting the order of God is only temporary. Never think of burying yourself when there's still so much more life to live.

Moses's first attempt to relieve God's people failed when it was attempted in his own strength. Moses knew he had purpose, but he did not have the proper training for the mission of delivering God's people. Whenever you have purpose without training, it creates room for failure. Know the difference between your strength and God's. Don't try to do this in your own strength. Individuals who have purpose but lack proper training have destroyed many people. Corporate training is extremely important. When you're sent, you will not have to war in order to defeat anyone. Anything that opposes you when you have the rod in your hand has walked into unknown defeat.

When you carry the rod, God wars against your enemy and not you. Exodus 17:9-10 (NKJV) says this:

And Moses said to Joshua, "Choose us some men and go out, fight with Amalek. Tomorrow I will stand on the top of the hill with the rod of God in my hand." So Joshua did as Moses said to him, and fought with Amalek. And Moses, Aaron, and Hur went up to the top of the hill.

As you carry the rod of God—which is symbolic of His authority and power—He will continue to fight for you. Never become discouraged when an enemy does not repent or say "I'm sorry." God has another plan for that situation. He is making you a deliverer and sending His power and authority to you. The power and authority are needed, because you will face more than one enemy. The same rod that delivered you the first time will deliver you every time. God has given you a man of God in the earth who represents a rod of truth in the house. By upholding his hands through your support, you help to strengthen your man of God and in return gain more and more victories.

NOTES

CHAPTER 4

POWER FROM WITHIN

There shall come forth a Rod from the stem of Jesse,

and a Branch shall grow out of his roots. The Spirit

of the LORD *shall rest upon Him, the Spirit of wisdom*

and understanding, the Spirit of counsel and might,

the Spirit of knowledge and of the fear of the LORD.

Isaiah 11:1-2 (NKJV)

Then a Shoot (the Messiah) will spring from the stock

of Jesse [David's father], and a Branch from his roots

will bear fruit. And the Spirit of the LORD *will rest on*

Him—the Spirit of wisdom and understanding, the Spirit

of counsel and strength, the Spirit of knowledge and

of the [reverential and obedient] fear of the LORD—"

Isaiah 11:1-2 (AMP)

G od's plan from the beginning was to release His kingdom power so that man would be able to govern the earth like God governs heaven. He wants to rule from the inner core of your being and influence the earth through you. God always works from the inside of man, even while man chooses to work from the outside in. We understand that man looks at the outward appearance, but God looks at the heart (1 Samuel 16:7). Man begins the search with the appearance so that the spirit will not be changed. God begins with the spirit and, over time, your outward appearance begins to change. God's way of doing things is more productive than man's.

Jesus was the Rod that came through Jesse's son King David. Once we understand the ark of the Covenant, the

Ten Commandments, the manna, and the rod of Aaron, we will function in limitless power as believers. All these items were located in the ark of the covenant, which gave the ark power from within. The Word of God works from within your heart. The stronger your heart is through the Word of God, the more it limits your mind from overruling the laws of God. As we explored earlier, the rod was a scepter of rule and authority that was carried by kings and leaders. The rod in the hand of a king or leader represented his scepter.

A scepter represents royal or imperial power or authority—sovereignty. What you are carrying gives you power and authority, regardless of whether others around you believe it. What God has placed in you will manifest, so don't put a time limit on it. It's time to embrace your identity so God will bring the manifestation of His power. What was once an image in your mind can and will be physically seen by others. What you cannot see inwardly becomes difficult to see outwardly. Those who can believe it in a short period of time will see it outwardly. People cannot devalue you when God is enriching you. So believe in the power that has been placed within you, and never let anyone cheapen you.

THE WORD OF GOD WORKS
FROM WITHIN YOUR HEART.
THE STRONGER YOUR HEART IS
THROUGH THE WORD OF GOD, THE
MORE IT LIMITS YOUR MIND FROM
OVERRULING THE LAWS OF GOD.

It's important to carry yourself as a person of value. When you do, others will treat you with respect. You'll know when you're arriving when you hear the phrase, "Who do you think you are?" Those in your presence will know there is something greater in you than where you are right now. It's only when they challenge who you are that you know you're

on the right track. God will always put a *yes* in your spirit,
regardless of how many *no*'s you have around you. Every *no*
is an announcement that you have aligned yourself with the
wrong friends. It's time for new people to come into your
life, because iron sharpens iron (Proverbs 27:17). Always
understand that wrong relationships and faulty communi-
cation will cause you to be dull in your sensitivity.

"And I will give you shepherds according to My heart,
who will feed you with knowledge and understanding.
Then it shall come to pass, when you are multiplied
and increased in the land in those days," says the LORD,
"that they will say no more, 'The ark of the covenant
of the LORD.*' It shall not come to mind, nor shall they*
remember it, nor shall they visit it, nor shall it be made
anymore." —Jeremiah 3:15-16 (NKJV)

You have to reconsider the negativity you may have
heard about prosperity preachers. In His provision, God
has given shepherds you can believe in and trust. God

removed the ark and exchanged it for shepherds. As long as the ark was among the children of Israel, they won the battle. As long as you adhere to the words of your shepherd, you will win some of the battles. The ark could not verbally communicate, but your shepherd can.

Hebrews 9:4 (NKJV) reads,

> . . . which had the golden censer and the ark of the covenant overlaid on all sides with gold, in which were the golden pot that had the manna, Aaron's rod that budded, and the tablets of the covenant . . .

As we see in scripture, these items were transferred into the shepherd-leader by God. The shepherd will share with you things that will cause you to be victorious in life. The shepherd is never exempt from victory, because he holds the rod or scepter. A real shepherd knows they only exist because God's people need miracles in their lives.

Men and women of God should represent the ark of the covenant and what it contained. It is not possible for you to starve when God has sent a shepherd that feeds you with knowledge and understanding. God's original intent was for everyone to have a shepherd, because the shepherd represents God with you. Miracles will be the norm in your life when you know that God has someone representing Him on earth.

The Rod that was Jesus now lives in the born-again believer. Jesus was the Rod and the Word existing in human form. When we ask Jesus into our hearts, everything that was in the ark now lives inside of us. You are a powerful person and you must make a decision to believe it. When you become born again, another tenant comes to live in your heart, which means you are not alone. A King is now living inside of you, which means you are now a king under a King. It's time to stop living beneath your privileges and your past. Rise up with your scepter and declare that you are royalty.

There is a difference between Jesus being *around* you and Jesus ruling *within* you. He rules within you! With this type of authority, you can rule over your oppressor. Every form of oppression that has been utilized by negative influences is now subject to you. John 14:11-12 (NKJV) contains the words of Jesus:

> *"Believe Me that I am in the Father and the Father in Me, or else believe Me for the sake of the works themselves. Most assuredly, I say to you, he who believes in Me, the works that I do he will do also; and greater works than these he will do, because I go to My Father."*

Jesus has declared in this scripture what God declared in Genesis 1:26. You are created to rule, subdue and take dominion because Jesus lives inside of you. There is no force of darkness that can stop you from operating in victory if you believe it. You shall do greater works and break the back of poverty.

NOTES

CHAPTER 5

ARISE, JUMP, AND DISMANTLE!

So Moses went and returned to Jethro his father-in-law, and said to him, "Please let me go and return to my brethren who are in Egypt, and see whether they are still alive." And Jethro said to Moses, "Go in peace." Now the LORD said to Moses in Midian, "Go, return to Egypt; for all the men who sought your life are dead."

Exodus 4:18-19 (NKJV)

T he spirit of God is still working; He just needs you to be an agent through which He can work. Those who

are going to deliver the people are authorized both spiri-
tually and physically. Those who are sent have no reason
to flee or be afraid.

". . . saying, "Arise, take the young Child and His
mother, and go to the land of Israel, for those who sought
the young Child's life are dead." —Matthew 2:20 (NKJV)

Arise, the influences that have threatened your
well-being have been removed. You cannot remain in
the past, because it will keep you from responding to
God's direction for now. It's time to get beyond your emotional hurdles. God will send you back to the place that
posed a threat to you. Your past may become your min-
istry—if you're willing to pick it up by the tail. You will
become a great support to the purpose to which you have
been assigned.

You have every right to expect greatness when you're
in the position to achieve it. The very thing you fled
from—no matter what the reason—you now have the

strength to conquer. No one is ever afraid of leadership; they are afraid of the character of the one that abused them. You have a tendency to fear in the present because of unresolved issues in the past. I believe the thing that has threatened you has lost its influence over you. It's your job to be a deliverer to those who are dealing with it now.

YOU CANNOT REMAIN IN THE PAST, BECAUSE IT WILL KEEP YOU FROM RESPONDING TO GOD'S DIRECTION FOR NOW.

Your opposition attacks you because of the way you think, they don't understand you were created with a purpose. When your way of thinking changes, you can grab everything that has been disruptive by the tail. God will send you back to places where He has already dismantled their disruptive power. He will never send you back if He had not already done the work. God does the work and you get the benefits. You will never enjoy the benefits of triumph until you understand that God has already dismantled your opposition.

"Having disarmed principalities and powers, He made a public spectacle of them, triumphing over them in it."
—*Colossians 2:15*

When spiritual opposition is disarmed, we will experience a physical victory. The things we can't see have more power than the things we can see. The things that have dominated us have been disarmed by Jesus. Stop trying to get physical victory without getting spiritual victory first. Consistent, daily prayer will strengthen you for spiritual victory. Many of our challenges come out of the spirit realm, which is unseen. Don't be offended by people that try to block you—that is a sign that the spirit realm of darkness is intimidated by you.

The principalities of this world are designed to work against you. They infiltrate the minds of people not focused on the future. Much of your opposition has risen from an attack on someone else's mind. It's not wise to think you only have outward opposition—you are battling the inward thoughts of others. We realize COVID-19 is a spiritual enemy that provokes us to fear. Fear has the ability to enhance your spiritual enemy—that's why God has not given us a spirit of fear, according to 2 Timothy 1:7.

If you did not win the battle the first round, it is because God had not removed the protection from your opposition.

If the LORD delights in us, then He will bring us into this land and give it to us, 'a land which flows with milk and honey.' Only do not rebel against the LORD, nor fear the people of the land, for they are our bread; their protection has departed from them, and the LORD is with us. Do not fear them.

> *"If the LORD delights in us, then He will bring us into this land and give it to us, 'a land which flows with milk and honey.' Only do not rebel against the LORD, nor fear the people of the land, for they are our bread; their protection has departed from them, and the LORD is with us. Do not fear them." —Numbers 14:8-9 (NKJV)*

This pandemic has been a challenge, but it has disarmed systems that have kept us out of God's best. We will eat and enjoy while we possess what God has given us. Anything that is going to remain is not achieved quickly, so don't give up when it's a slow process. The longer it takes, the more mature you become, and the more you are able to obtain the massive blessing God has for you. God does not use a microwave; your blessing is oven-baked, which means it has taken time.

We are coming into a season where those who possess our inheritance cannot stop us from taking hold of it. When principalities and powers sense you moving forward, they align themselves against you. Don't allow darkness to get in the way of what God has promised you and what you will possess. You're coming into a season in which the enemy cannot stop you. All his attempts to strike you only elevate you. When he tried to push you out, he pushed you in. Everything that was meant for evil against you God has turned for your good, according to Genesis 50:20. You can't tell everyone about your dream, because the enemy is listening to the conversation you have with God. Do not worry—they may take your coat, but they cannot take the favor of God from your life.

NOTES

CHAPTER 6

EXPECT GREAT RESULTS

Then he called for Moses and Aaron by night, and said,

"Rise, go out from among my people, both you and the

children of Israel. And go, serve the LORD as you have

said. Also take your flocks and your herds, as you have

said, and be gone; and bless me also." And the Egyptians

urged the people, that they might send them out of the

land in haste. For they said, "We shall all be dead."

So the people took their dough before it was leavened,

having their kneading bowls bound up in their clothes

on their shoulders. Now the children of Israel had done

according to the word of Moses, and they had asked

from the Egyptians articles of silver, articles of gold, and

*clothing. And the L*ORD *had given the people favor in the*

sight of the Egyptians, so that they granted them what

they requested. Thus they plundered the Egyptians."

Exodus 12:31-36 (NKJV)

For everything God does, He supplies a roadmap to ensure we reach our destination. Whenever your God-given leadership is declaring the Word over your life, it is in order to get you to your destination. The Word of God helps increase your belief for what is promised to you.

You may be facing situations that counterattack the things for which you are believing. God is going to bring deliverance in every area. It took 430 years for deliverance to come to the children of Israel. They continued to communicate the word of deliverance from generation to generation. Your Bible is the best roadmap to a great kingdom life. Continue to pass the information of the

Word to those who come after you. Don't die until you have passed it on. It's important that you keep on talking about God's promises from one generation to the next.

Many of God's promises were canceled in one generation because those people did not believe enough to pass them on to the next generation. You must speak in faith to keep God's promise alive. Tell every generation that a better day is coming. There is a generation that will see the manifestation of what you have said. You cannot stay poor when God says it's a season to be wealthy. If God set it up, no man can change it. No one is going to be able to interrupt your breakthrough in this season. The time has come.

Expect These Results When You Take the Serpent by the Tail:

A miraculous deliverance will come after many years of captivity. When you have been bound for so long, it will take a miracle from God to bring your freedom. We cannot be deceived by what true freedom looks like. The pressure to drive certain types of cars and live in certain neighborhoods can also represent bondage. Being able to shop around at the mall or purchase nice things is not a sign of freedom if it leads to debt. If you're driving to the mall and spending all the money meant for your utilities, that represents captivity. You're in bondage when you feel that you have to look a certain way to impress other people. The pressure to drive certain types of cars and live in certain neighborhoods can represent bondage. It is good to have the proper degree and training for the career you have chosen, but do not allow it to put you in bondage. Attending a large church is not a sign of acceptance. Don't allow people to create another situation of bondage for you. No matter how long you have been in bondage to things, now is the time to know that you can be free. God's assurance for freedom is here for everyone. God desires us all to worship Him in freedom. We no longer have to think like slaves.

YOU MUST SPEAK IN FAITH TO KEEP GOD'S PROMISE ALIVE. TELL EVERY GENERATION THAT A BETTER DAY IS COMING.

You are going to come out healthy and wealthy because the system was holding your blessing. Your moment will be filled with so many miracles that sickness will not be found in your house. Prepare your mind to handle the good things being transferred to you. Many of you are too young to retire, but you're never too young to be wealthy. This is not the time to try it out—it is the time to believe it. This is not just a great idea—this is God's idea. The thing that was once hurting you was also holding your blessing.

Now that you're truly free from the hurt, the blessing is yours. No longer think about the days of slavery. You need that mental space to plan for the land you're possessing. No matter how much the past has affected you mentally—either by counseling or a miracle—you will go free. Much of what belongs to you was close to you the entire time, but you were not able to process the fact that it was yours. You should never expose a person to greatness and then tell them they can't have it. *You can have it because it is yours.*

What you feared will be completely destroyed for following you.

Now it came to pass, in the morning watch, that the LORD looked down upon the army of the Egyptians through the pillar of fire and cloud, and He troubled the army of the Egyptians. And He took off their chariot wheels, so that they drove them with difficulty; and the Egyptians said, "Let us flee from the face of Israel, for the L<small>ORD</small> *fights for them against the Egyptians."*

—*Exodus 14:24-25, (NKJV)*

If there is an enemy that has not turned back from pursuing you, God's plan is to get the glory for that final victory. Pharaoh chasing the children of Israel was God's opportunity to show the world how powerful He was, and He will do the same in your life. Our personal strength is seen when we're facing something that seems strong enough to overthrow us. In the end, we maintain the victory. The enemy that followed you into 2020—which is a brand-new decade—will be like the chariots of Pharaoh that began to lose their wheels. God has always maintained space between His people and their enemies. Just like the waters of the Red Sea, when the enemy thinks he is closing in on you, he will be overcome. God has slowed down your opposition to get you to the other side so the enemy of fear will share the same fate as the Egyptians: they saw them no more.

NOTES

OTHER BOOKS BY THE AUTHOR

"10 Years of Unprecedented Peace, Favor & Abundance"

"Words to Inspire You to Dream"

"I AM THE ONE"

"Just Beyond Grief"

FOR MORE ABOUT THE AUTHOR

WEBSITE: WWW.STEPHENADAVIS.ORG

EMAIL: INFO@DIRECTCONNECTINC.ORG

FACEBOOK: @STEPHENADAVIS

INSTAGRAM: @STEPHENADAVIS